Fiery Tales
by
Peter Wolf

Illustrations by Paul King

Typeset in Times New Roman

ISBN-978 1898368 05 2

Pre-press and production by
Richard d'Alton of 147design

Printed and bound by
Latimer Trend, Plymouth,
Devon PL6 7PY

I am very pleased to have been given the opportunity to write a few words for Peter's book of funny and light hearted Fire Service stories some of which I admit I have played a small part in the role of acting the fool. Some unkind Managers might say, no change there then.

This book has been Peter's labour of love, taking him many hours of humorous banter with colleagues throughout the service and beyond, a task willingly undertaken with the support of the talented cartoonist Paul King and Peter's family and friends.

I have personally been involved with the Firefighters fund, formally the Firefighters National Benevolent fund in one role or another for some 34 years.

Through the purchase of this book, two very worthwhile charities will benefit by receiving a proportion of the profits, namely the Firefighters charity, and the Help the Hero's fund. Like so many excellent charities, they rely totally on public donations and the sale of goods and books like Peter's to help and assist so many people in real need.

The Fire Service National Benevolent fund, as it was formally called, was created in 1943 to deal with the hardship arising from the Second World War and continues today as a lasting memorial to the Firemen and Firewomen who lost their lives during that war.

Since the end of the Second World War, there has been a need to care for those orphaned or widowed during the war and they have been joined by a steady stream of recipients including widows and orphans of those who have died more recently.

In addition to this early support, the Fund stands today to provide a wide range of benefits to all serving/retired Firefighters/Control and support staff and their families. These include convalescing, following accident or injury/illness and intensive therapy treatments and financial assistance where necessary.

On behalf of the charities benefitting from the proceeds of this book, I wish it the success it deserves.

Dave Crawford

Red Watch Torquay

ACKNOWLEDGEMENTS

There are so many people to thank for helping me in the compilation of this book that I am not sure where to start, but I must try:

Firstly, all the friends and firefighters who have allowed me to use their stories in this book. There would not be a book without them.

Nadine Watson, a firefighter and friend at Paignton fire station for helping me with a lot of the typing in the early stages, and more latterly helping me with all the e-mails and attachments that I am so hopeless at.

Matthew Clarke at Torbay Books for his help and advice in getting the book from print and onto the shelf.

My fellow green watch members and big Gary Kingsley for holding my considerable weight in the front cover photograph!

Christine Willis for her fantastic graphic design work on the book cover.

John Cowley for stepping in at the last minute and correcting a huge number of my spelling and punctuation mistakes.

Richard d'Alton for his clever pre-press layout of the book.

My brother, Michael Wolf for his help in promoting the book.

Wendy Hawkins for all her support and expertise in the creating of the website.

Last but by no means least my hugely supportive family. Irene and my two daughters Sam and Jo have always been there encouraging me to get the job done, and putting up with 'Mr. Grumpy' when he has had writers block or a serious bout of 'technophobia'!

Thank you all so much.

THE FOREWORD

I have been in the Fire Service now for about 23 years, and for the most part have enjoyed it tremendously. My original reasons for wanting to join included some of the following. Firstly I hoped that the Fire Service might turn out to be more interesting and challenging than my previous job, and this certainly proved to be the case. Secondly there was an altruistic hope that I might be able to help those in need or in danger, and this on more than one occasion, as part of a team I would like to think that I have achieved. Thirdly like many younger men, I hoped the Fire Service might provide some excitement. On several occasions it has lived up to those expectations, to the extent, on one or three occasions I have thought that things have been getting a little too exciting! What I did not realise then, that along with the excitement, there would be some long periods of inactivity, when things were not so stimulating. I was soon to find out however, that Firefighters are quite good at providing their own entertainment, of which more later.

What I do think in those early and eager days, was that I never expected quite so much humour within the watches or quite so many humorous situations to develop either out on calls or simply in the work place. It will definitely be the friendship, the camaraderie and the humour that will be best remembered when they put me out to grass in a few years time. It is the humour and the funny situations that I have encountered that I am going to try and share with you now through my compilation of short stories.

I have certainly enjoyed talking to friends and colleagues whilst reminiscing over some of the funnier moments we have experienced. In my search for a good story I have also been lucky enough to meet some great characters from other brigades. The immediate bond between us always seeming to be a similar sense of humour. Many that I have talked to have agreed with me there was more outrageous humour in times gone by, possibly something to do with the more outrageous and eccentric characters that were in the service back then. Certainly the tidal wave of Health and Safety and political correctness would make it less likely that many of these situations could develop again. Perhaps having read some of the stories many of you might think that may be just as well. However these things have all happened in one Fire Service or another and I hope that you will enjoy the humour herein.

I must emphasise that the purpose of this book is in no way to denigrate the Fire Service or the fantastic work that it does for so much of the time. Nor am I trying to make any particular individual or individuals look foolish. Here I think we will all appreciate the reality that if I were only to write about fires or rescues which all went without a hitch, this would be a much less interesting and certainly a much less humorous read. The truth of the matter is, that what we in the Fire Service do is far from an exact science and in many situations we are a long way from being in control of either the characters or the circumstances that we find ourselves having to deal with, hence the possibility for any number of outcomes from any given situation.

PART 1: 'COCK-UPS'

THE TRACTOR

THE PIGS

LONDON BRIDGE AND FALLING DOWN

NOT A WHITE CHRISTMAS

A CAT WITH EIGHT LIVES

I ONLY TOLD YOU TO KNOCK DOWN THE BLOODY DOOR!

MAKING AN IMPRESSION

A ROYAL NAVAL COCK-UP!

HANG ON TO THAT HANDBRAKE

NEVER FEAR THE FIRE SERVICE IS HERE

ON THIN ICE

A LOCK-UP COCK-UP!

A BATHROOM BREAK-IN

RAISING THE ROOF

Fiery Tales

THE TRACTOR

This was the first story I heard that involved a massive Fire Service 'cock-up' and the story that made me think that I should write them down. Paul's depiction of the event is also my favourite and therefore it must be the first story in the book.

Before I start on the story proper, I must first explain a little bit about barn-fires. Most firefighters I know enjoy going to a good fire. It isn't that we want to see anyone hurt or property destroyed, far from it, but it is what we are trained to deal with, there is always a bit of adrenaline involved, and we derive huge satisfaction from a successful outcome. However, very few firefighters, especially the more experienced ones, will be very enthusiastic about a barn-fire, because they are extremely predictable, they usually take for ever to put out, and they entail hours of straightforward hard manual labour. Once a barn-fire takes hold, which is very quickly, it does not matter how much water is put on it, the fire just spreads deeper into the straw. Therefore the only way they can be completely extinguished is by pulling the straw apart and damping down every bit. Not only does this take hours, but after a fire all the straw will be rendered useless anyway, so the whole process always seems to be very futile.

The only saving grace in some barn-fires is a helpful farmer, with a tractor and a hydraulic fork-lift on the front, who doesn't mind getting stuck in and helping the crews pull the straw out of the barn, one chunk at a time, making it much easier to damp down and saving hours of drudgery with a pitch-fork. This was the case in the eastern area of our county, where a large barn was what we call 'well-alight' and the farmer was only too happy to help with his tractor. It was still taking a long time, but as he pulled out huge chunks of smouldering straw the crews outside simply had to pull apart and damp down each chunk as it came out rather than go in and get the straw out themselves with pitchforks.

Even with the help of the tractor, it was still taking a long time to get through all the straw, so when the farmer announced that he needed to go and milk the cows and suggested that the firefighters would have to finish off the job with pitchforks, an audible groan could be heard. Then one very obliging firefighter stepped forward and suggested that, as he had worked most of his life on a farm, he was sure he could carry on where the farmer had left off, drive the tractor and operate the hydraulic fork. As the tractor was nearly brand new, and presumably worth a lot of money, the farmer wanted to check that the firefighter could indeed operate the hydraulics. Our willing volunteer hopped up into the driving seat and showed that he could indeed operate the hydraulics very competently. The farmer therefore agreed that he could carry on with the tractor work while he went to milk his cows. The tired crews were delighted that they were not going to have to pull the straw out of the barn manually. However during this short break the straw had started to glow a little more brightly. The new driver drove back into the barn and deftly lifted a large chunk of straw that was now on fire. It was not his operation of the hydraulics that was the problem, but his operation of the gears, for try as he might he could not locate reverse gear. While he was desperately trying to put the tractor into reverse a large piece of burning straw fell on to the tractor. The lads outside did not react very quickly to the problem, resulting in the farmer not only losing his barn but his tractor as well!

Fiery Tales

THE PIGS

Following the tractor disaster, this is another story with farmyard over-tones, but this is less of a 'cock-up' and more a serious case of opening your mouth and putting your foot right in it!

The scene for this story is a fire in a pig farm, when an electric light fell into the straw in one of the pig enclosures. This started a small fire which threatened to develop into a much more serious one and put all the pigs at risk. The fire, although late in the evening, was discovered early and we were called in time to help the farmer get his terrified pigs out of the enclosure. You can picture the scene, farmer, firefighters, pigs and smoke, basically organised chaos.

As it was dark, portable lights were brought in from the fire appliances and placed on tripods around the building to help with fire fighting and the evacuation of the poor old pigs. The evacuation and fire fighting were going well, when a senior fire officer arrived. The role of a senior fire officer at an incident is to support the officer in charge, to check that all necessary measures have been taken, and to take over the incident if necessary. Just before he arrived one of the last pigs to be shooed out of the building knocked one of the tripods and light over so it was just lying in the straw. At the same time one of the policemen that had been outside helping with the traffic came in to see what was going on.

In summary, we have a smoky, badly lit building, now free of pigs, a senior officer looking to find a problem to put right, and a policeman. The senior officer, not understanding the events that had unfolded, saw the light on the floor and asked the officer in charge why the light was not up on the tripod.

"One of the pigs knocked it over, sir".

In what can only be described as a complete moment of madness the senior officer, all steamed up, went over to the policeman and asked: "Which one of you clumsy buggers did that, then?"

LONDON BRIDGE AND FALLING DOWN

A London firefighter told me this story. It happened many years ago, so I hope that nobody will get into trouble over it and that nobody will be offended by it. The crew involved were definitely negligent, and the outcome could have been much worse, but as no one was seriously hurt I feel that it is acceptable to include it.

In the past firefighters were responsible for checking that fire hydrants operated effectively. We spent many hours walking the streets, checking the hydrant pits and making sure that that the hydrants turn on and off easily. As I understand it, in London much the same thing happened, although our hydrants are only about two feet deep with a hydrant cover about one foot by eighteen inches, whereas in London the pits are about five feet deep and the covers about two feet square. The reason for these much larger pits in the city is that because of the huge volume of traffic the hydrants need to be much deeper to protect them from all the vibrations from the traffic.

On one this occasion a London crew were checking the hydrants on one of the London bridges. As I recall, after you have done several hydrants, a degree of complacency can often set in. So it must have been with this particular London crew. We have it instilled in us at training school to be very careful with hydrant plate covers. They should only be taken off at the last minute before use, never left unattended, and always put back immediately after use, for obvious reasons.

We are all human, however, and after the crew had removed the hydrant plate prior to inspection, they were distracted from their task by a boating accident under the bridge. Apparently a yacht had crossed in front of a barge, and to avoid it the barge had steered into one of the stanchions of the bridge. This caused a lot of noise and a lot of bad language to be uttered by the driver of the barge. The fire service crew rushed to the side of the bridge to see what was going on and to check that everyone was all right. They then got involved in a bit of banter with the guy on the barge, like cockneys do.

Unfortunately they had completely forgotten the uncovered hydrant pit, which was now a gaping hole in the pavement. Very unfortunately for them, there happened to be a blind man walking across the bridge with his white stick in his hand. He did not pick out the hole in the pavement and promptly disappeared into the hydrant pit. The crew were only aware of the poor man's predicament when they heard him shout and saw his white stick waving out of the top of the hydrant. Thankfully he was not too badly hurt, just a bit scratched and dazed by his unexpected fall. He was extremely cross, however, and rightly so, that someone had left an uncovered hole in the pavement!

The highly embarrassed crew rushed across to pull him out and dust him down. They were mightily relieved that he did not need an ambulance. He was almost totally blind, however, and could not see the fire appliance or who had been responsible for his fall. He asked who they were and for the telephone number of their manager so that he could put in a complaint. The officer in charge of the crew realised that he could be in some serious trouble and replied, "I'm very sorry, sir, it's British Telecom", and then gave him a ficticious number.

I very much hope this story does not offend any blind or disabled people. We as a service are very aware of the needs of the disabled and I could quote many instances where we have gone out of our way to assist the elderly and disabled. This was a genuine mistake, albeit a bad one, and the officer in charge should of course have owned up as to who they were. I would like to think that if he had been seriously injured the crew would have acted differently, and this story would not then have been included.

NOT A WHITE CHRISTMAS

Before telling this story, I must explain how we normally put out himney fires. Chimney fires only usually occur when chimneys are not swept regularly, allowing soot and resin to accumulate on the inside of the flue. This accumulation can catch fire, resulting in sparks shooting out of the chimney pot, and is often accompanied by the roaring sound of air being entrained into the hearth to feed the fire. When we arrive we first put handfuls of water onto the fire in the grate to extinguish it, and quite often the resultant steam going up the chimney is enough to put the chimney fire out too. However, with a more established chimney fire, we have to use chimney rods. These rods, which are each about a metre long, are linked ogether and forced slowly up the flue. The rods have a sprinkler on top of them, fed by a hose and attached to a simple hand pump that is put in a bucket of water. As the rods are forced up the chimney, a slow but steady sprinkle of water is usually enough to put the fire out. However, in some older buildings with multiple chimneys, this is not the case. Sometimes the flues are not straight enough and they interlink, making it very difficult to force the rods up the chimney. More drastic action is then needed, and the fire needs to be extinguished from above.

This was exactly the situation facing a friend of mine in a southern county brigade a few years back. His crew were called to an old people's retirement home in an old Victorian building, which had lots of chimneys, none of them straight! The open fire in the main living room was going very nicely, and six or seven elderly folk were sitting around it enjoying their sherry and mince pies. The officer in charge informed the residents that they would have to move back a little to allow his crew to work, but they were welcome to watch the proceedings if they wished. As explained, the crew splashed some water onto the fire to put it out. The steam was not enough, however, so they began to rod the flue. This was anything but a straightforward chimney, and they were unable to get the rods very far up, so the officer had little choice but to order two members of his crew onto the roof with a hose reel jet to try and extinguish the fire from above. Bearing in mind that we try to do as little damage as possible, they were careful not to blast too much water down the chimney.

A radio link was established between the fire fighters on the roof and the officer in the living room, who ordered them to carefully trickle some water down the chimney, having first put sheets around the hearth to protect the carpets. No water appeared down the chimney, but the fire had definitely not gone out. The boss, mindful of the fact that it was Christmas morning and that everyone wanted to get home to lunch, ordered the men on the roof to stop messing about and give the chimney a good blast. The old dears in the living room, naturally inquisitive, were enjoying the entertainment when the blast of water hit a big blockage of soot. As I tried to explain earlier, we protect the floor but do not sheet up the fireplace as a chimney sweep would because we normally try to prevent damage from water but not soot! As you have probably already guessed, a huge quantity of soot fell down the chimney and billowed out into the living room. It was a shame that the residents had not been taken out of the room first as, when my friend walked back into the room, all that could see of the elderly onlookers was the whites of their eyes!

A CAT WITH EIGHT LIVES

We frequently get called out for all sorts of animal rescues, although it is mostly seagulls and cats. Usually the RSPCA calls us, when a seagull is tangled in some wire on a roof or a cat has climbed somewhere very high and the owner is worried about it. The RSPCA do not have long ladders, hence our involvement. We sometimes attend dogs trapped underground, or birds in chimneys, and more rarely again larger farm animals stuck in bogs or trapped in a variety of different places.

This story relates to a classic cat up a tree, and the RSPCA had called us because the cat was fully 40 feet up the tree and had been there so long that the owner was worried about it. The longest ladder on most appliances is a 135 ladder, which means it is 13.5 metres or roughly 40 feet long when fully extended. That is how I know that the cat was 40 feet up, because even when fully extended the ladder could only just reach it. Sometimes the RSPCA officers go up the ladder themselves, as they are the experts in animal husbandry, but quite often, especially when it is really high, we go up ourselves with gloves on to protect us from pecks and bites. In this instance it was a young firefighter called Gary who went up the ladder to rescue the cat, which appeared to be stuck.

If you can imagine from the cat's perspective, if you have been happily minding your own business lying in the sunshine up a tree, and a large yellow-helmeted human being turns up unexpectedly, it must be a bit frightening. Anyway, when Gary got up to the cat, it took fright and promptly tried to escape from its would-be rescuer by going round to the other side of the tree. Now Gary, who was already right at the top of the ladder and at full stretch, had to reach round the tree and try to grope for the cat. Unfortunately the combination of the scared cat and Gary's outstretched attempts to grab it resulted in the cat falling fully 40 feet to the ground. Luckily there were two or three thin branches in the descent that helped to break the fall slightly, but to the consternation of the owners and all involved the poor cat still hit the ground pretty hard. However the fact that he was able to shake himself down and run off after such a fall gives credence to the old saying about a cat having nine lives. Apparently the cat was so shaken up by events that he didn't return home for five days.

I ONLY TOLD YOU TO KNOCK DOWN THE BLOODY DOOR!!!

One of the many types of incident we can be called out to is a gas explosion. These do not happen very often, and in all honesty after an explosion all we can do is search for survivors, and try and make an unstable situation as safe as possible prior to re-construction.

I remember the very sad case of a little girl who was walking past a house on her way to school, when the wall of the house was blown out by a gas explosion. The wall landed right on top of her and she was crushed by the sheer weight of it.

The following story, related to me by an ex-London firefighter, did not have quite such terrible consequences, just very serious and potentially very embarrassing ones! Apparently an elderly lady in her house in London had turned on the gas fire but failed to ignite it. Not being aware of this she lit a cigarette a few minutes later and ignited the gas. The room exploded blowing out the windows and some of the internal walls. My friend was one of the crew who were mobilised to the incident. As the explosion had already taken place, there was not much danger to the firefighters apart from the falling masonry, and the priority was to find the elderly lady, who had not come out of the house.

When they arrived at the house the front door was either locked or jammed from the blast, so the officer in charge ordered the door to be forced open. Sometimes when people are trapped in a room, and we know they are not in any danger, there is time to remove the door jambs and force the door with as little damage as possible. However, in an emergency like this the door is simply forced as fast as possible, usually by the largest member of the crew putting a shoulder or boot to the door. In this instance the door was shouldered and crashed in off its hinges, top first. The firefighters rushed in over the smashed door to be greeted by a scene of devastation, glass bricks dust and debris, but where was the old lady? When they retraced their steps they were embarrassed to find her under the door they had just trampled over!

Luckily she was still semi conscious, so she was pulled out, dusted down and carefully stretchered out to the waiting ambulance. Hopefully she was too mesmerised by the blast to realise that she had been under the door that six hefty firefighters had rushed over in their attempt to save her!

MAKING AN IMPRESSION

The Fire Officer who told me this story was, at the time, a very xperienced sub officer, but he had just been transferred to a different station in Plymouth where he was keen to make a good impression on the fire fighters he was going to be in charge of. He was usually very good at his job, and a more conscientious and practical fire fighter would be hard to find. However, we all have our off days, and fire fighting being the inexact science that it is we can be caught out from time to time. If the officer, who we shall call Des, was trying to make an impression, this he certainly managed to do.

When you look for the reasons for a 'cock up,' it is all too easy to look for someone or something other than yourself to blame. However, thinking about the story, there were probably three reasons for everything going 'pear shaped.' Firstly, not knowing your crew doesn't help. Secondly luck, or lack of it, in any given circumstance always plays a part. The third reason is more complicated and needs a little explanation. The officer concerned had recently come back from a course where he had been given instruction on the use of a relatively new piece of equipment, namely a positive pressure ventilation fan. This may sound like a highly technical piece of machinery, but is in fact just a large fan that, in simple terms, we set up outside a building to blow smoke out of it. As this fan introduces huge quantities of fresh air, and therefore oxygen, into the building, it has to be used with extreme care as, if used incorrectly, it can very much work against fire fighting operations. The officer concerned in this incident will have none of these excuses offered, and he thinks all that befell him was of his own making, but please feel free to make up your own minds.

Des had not been long on his new watch when they were called to a fire in the roof space of a fourth floor flat. The flat was in a terrace of houses in Lipsom Road, Plymouth, one of many houses of multiple occupation (HIMOs) in the area. HIMOs are not always the best maintained or looked after properties, if you understand what I mean. This was a December day, and an icy one at that, and the owner of the flat was up in his roof space, getting down his Christmas tree and decorations. He was rummaging around, when his friend from the third floor flat called him down for a Christmas drink, which turned out to be a whole bottle of whisky between them. We know this because the owner of the fourth floor flat was almost legless when the fire service arrived. A halogen lamp, which he had been using for illumination, had fallen over and started the fire in all the rubbish in his roof space.

Des thought this was a chance to show his crew all that he knew. He ordered the two hose-reels on each side of the appliance to be joined together and dragged to the fourth floor of the building by a breathing apparatus team. So far so good, but unfortunately the hatch to the roof space was only built for small people to get through and certainly not for large fire fighters with breathing apparatus on. Des suggested that one of the team should put his head through the hatch and use the hose-reel jet, pretty much above his head, to try and put the fire out. After doing the best he could from above his head, the firefighter in the breathing apparatus set appeared to have put the fire out. Des put his head through the hatch and, using his torch, couldn't see any flames, but the roof space was heavily smoke logged. Then, with the brainwave that was the undoing of everything, he ordered the PPV (positive pressure ventilation) to be set up to clear the smoke. The breathing apparatus team were on their way down with the hose-reel and the PPV was put to work. Unfortunately the fire was not quite out, the air being blown into the roof space reignited an ember and very quickly the fire took hold again. Fires in roofs can be notoriously difficult and quickly get out of hand, especially if they get through to an adjoining roof space. Des was now suddenly picturing the worst case scenario of a terrace of houses with all the roofs alight, and shouted down for the breathing apparatus team and the hose reel to return as fast as possible! One thing I did not tell you about the PPV is that it makes a hell of a noise, and he was not heard above this noise. His crew had gone back to the appliances and were now in relaxed mode. Des had his second officer with him, so yelled at him to get a bucket of water from the kitchen to try and douse the flames until the BA team got back. They managed a couple of bowls between them while they are waiting for the team (who were not on their way) and then, in a moment of madness, Des decided to get up into the roof space himself to throw a bowl of water a little bit further back. As he got into the roof he slipped off one of the beams and one leg went right through the ceiling so that he was stuck fast. At the same time, he and his number two realised that help was not on the way, so the second officer ran downstairs to get help fire fighting and to get Des out of the ceiling plaster.

The second officer ran outside for reinforcements, forgetting the icy conditions, and slipped flat on his back in the road. So at this point we have the officer in charge stuck in the roof and the second officer on his back in the road! It was worse than that, because for a brief period, Des could only breathe fresh air by contorting himself and getting his head out of the hatch. This was so difficult that he was actually breathing in more smoke than he should have been, and was sick all over the contents of the roof space. As you can imagine, this was not quite the impression he was trying to make with his new watch!

After most fires of any consequence we usually have a debrief when any points of view can be raised as to how an incident could have been dealt with more efficiently. To his eternal credit, Des looked at the lads on the debrief and said, with a completely straight face, 'I was just showing you all how not to deal with a fire so that we can all get it right next time.' They all fell about laughing at his admission of the cock up. He got many chances in ensuing years to show the men that he was actually a very good officer, but he told me that none of them had forgotten their first fire call together. In fact, I know that it is often brought up in conversation when the watch go out for a drink together, despite Des having asked them not to talk about it. I am just glad that after all these years he could enjoy relating the story to me and was able to laugh about himself.

A ROYAL NAVAL COCK-UP

I was told this story by a good friend of mine, who is now a senior officer in our Fire-Service and was formerly an officer in the Royal Navy. He was officer in charge when his watch had to attend a small kitchen fire in the Officers mess at H.M.S Drake, a land-based 'ship' in Plymouth's Devonport dockyard. This should have been a very routine turnout, were it not for the fact that the driver of the hydraulic platform always insisted on wearing his fire helmet even when he was driving. "You never know when you might hit something, buy" (which is the Plymouth translation for boy), he used to say. It may have made him safer, but it didn't improve his all-round vision!

Back to H.M.S. Drake, where at the time of the fire staff were extremely busy preparing the 'ship' for some very important guests who were arriving that night. It transpired that some admirals and home office big-wigs were going to meet their Brazilian counterparts at H.M.S. Drake to hand over the keys to a British Naval frigate they were selling. In true naval tradition everything was being scrubbed and polished to make the base look as 'ship-shape' and smart as possible for the important visitors. Everything that could have been painted or polished was gleaming and the grass had been cut, combed and waxed to perfection!

The officer in charge of the base on that day had no time for fires, even small ones, and not much more for the firefighters whose duty it was to attend them. As soon as our officer realised that it was safe and under control he started to order the other appliances back to the fire station, the first to go being the hydraulic platform. Before I try to explain what happened next, I must just point out to those of you with no naval knowledge, that everything that is important on a naval ship, even a land based one, takes place on the quarter-deck. Flags are raised, orders are given, and in olden times transgressors would be told what savage punishment they could look forward to. The quarterdeck here was very impressive and surrounded by an ornate stone balustrade wall, with large pillars on each corner and decorative capping stones jutting out from the top of each!

The Navy Officer in charge (the Jimmy) was proudly surveying the efforts of his men, when the top of the hydraulic platform driven by our poorly-sighted firefighter collided with one end of the capping stones sticking out from the top of a corner pillar. Much like a scene from a cartoon the pillar collapsed, pushing over the two walls connected to it, so that they fell like dominoes, each pillar knocking the next one down and so on all the way around the quarter-deck. The Fire Service officer received an urgent message telling him to go to the quarterdeck. The driver was still in the cab, surrounded by irate naval personnel, and he swore blind that he had not hit the wall. It only took a few seconds to realise what had happened. The driver's helmet was acting like a sunscreen and had blocked out his high level vision. As he had passed close to the pillar he hadn't seen the capping stone jutting out, and it was hit by the roof of the fire engine, leaving a deep gouge in the body work!

The very smart quarterdeck now looked more like a Spanish galleon after a battle during the Armada. The 'Jimmy' was beside himself with rage, and when he recovered his voice said to our officer, "If Sir Francis Drake was here today, that driver would be hanging from that yard-arm, and you would be hanging along side him". To his eternal credit our officer could only reply, "In the absence of Sir Francis Drake, please accept my apologies, and here are our insurance papers!"

HANG ON TO THAT HANDBRAKE!

This is a very simple story, which I think everyone can relate to. It may even have happened to some of you, but it should definitely not have happened to a Fire Appliance!

From time to time we get asked by members of the public to help do jobs that they cannot do themselves, such as hanging up banners or posters for charitable events, and having the ladders and the man-power, if we have the time, we are only too happy to oblige. On this specific occasion we were asked by the local council if we could help fill some duck-ponds in the local park, as they were drying out during a long (if somewhat rare in the south-west) period of hot, dry weather. Again, having the pumps and the manpower, how could we say no… poor old ducks, getting dry, muddy bottoms! The task itself was not too difficult as the duck ponds in question are only about 150 metres from the sea, albeit you have to walk under a narrow railway bridge to get to the beach. As the narrow railway bridge prevented us from taking the Fire Appliance down to the water's edge, the boys had to carry a portable pump down to the beach and then pump the water up through a few lengths of hose to the ponds. As a small point of interest we call this pump a 'light portable pump', which I have never understood as it's one of the heaviest things we ever carry in the Fire Service, apart from possibly another human being. However, I digress.

Having parked on a slope by the ponds, the driver of the appliance put the hand brake on and everyone dismounted. As it was quite a warm day the officer in charge of the appliance left his fire-tunic in the front of the cab between his seat and the driver's. He and the crew then got on with the task in hand until it started to rain. The officer in charge then went back to the appliance to get his fire-tunic, and as the driver's door was closer he reached up from that side to get his tunic. Unfortunately, as it was on the other side of the handbrake, he had to pull it over the brake handle to retrieve it, and in so doing he pulled the brake out of the 'park' position. As he walked back to where the others were working, he was horrified to see the Fire Appliance rolling back past him. He tried to get into the driver's seat and stop the runaway vehicle, but this is a difficult and dangerous manoeuvre and, try as he might, the appliance was heading for the ponds. So, having set out with the best of intentions to fill the ponds with sea water, one pond was sadly now filled with a Fire Appliance instead!

NEVER FEAR, THE FIRE SERVICE IS HERE!

Following on from the unfortunate story of the Fire Appliance in the duck-pond, here is another handbrake related tale.

Every year we get called to quite a lot of car fires, many of them caused by genuine electrical problems in the engine, but others caused deliberately by irresponsible idiots stealing and then 'torching' the stolen cars. Whatever the cause, once started car fires can burn ferociously and take a lot of extinguishing, as those of you who have experienced one will know. Car fires produce a lot of toxic and dangerous fumes, so we always wear full fire kit and the firefighters dealing with the fire will put on their breathing apparatus sets to avoid inhaling the fumes. Car fires can take place anywhere, from the garage at home (sadly I was present at a house fire started by the car in the garage when the house was completely destroyed, as it started at about 3 a.m.) to a totally remote location where it has been taken to be destroyed.

This story relates to a car parked on a slope in the middle of a busy town on the south coast, that caught fire accidentally. When the lads from the local station got there the car was burning quite well and had gathered a good-sized crowd of onlookers. They parked the appliance downhill from the car and the crew leapt into action. Breathing apparatus was donned, the hose-reels pulled off, pump engaged and the crew set about tackling the flames. The onlookers were very impressed by the efficiency of the crew. Unfortunately nobody had foreseen the brake-cable of the car burning through and the crowd were then much less impressed when the burning car started to roll back towards the fire appliance. I am told that out of desperation one of the firefighters even tried to battle with gravity and stop the car rolling. However it was a large car and a steep enough slope to make his task impossible, and he had to dive out of the way to avoid being pinned between car and fire engine. Chaos now ensued, as the lads not only had a burning car out of control, but potentially a Fire Appliance on fire too. I can only imagine that the crowd of spectators were by now far less impressed! We carry wheel chocks on all our appliances, which are generally used to ensure our own vehicles' safety on a slope. If only they had been used in this incident on the burning car, and in the previous story as well!

ON THIN ICE

This is only a short story, and I have probably only included it because of the quality of Paul's drawing. It could easily have had a different outcome. In fact it was a very narrow escape from a possible disaster. The incident only happened early in 2010, when we had some particularly cold weather, and was not exactly as portrayed in Paul's drawing. Nor were there any ducks involved this time.

During very cold, snowy weather snow chains are issued to all the appliances on each station. If it is deemed snowy or icy enough a snow chain is attached to each back wheel so that the appliance can still respond to emergency calls. As the chains slow the appliances down and are very bad for the tyres, there is always a big debate as to whether the chains should be attached or not, and they are generally only applied if the conditions are potentially dangerous. Of course the weather can change dramatically during the night, but as we are on south coast we rarely get conditions that warrant the chains.

On this occasion the chains had been left off on a night duty, as it was nowhere near freezing at midnight when the crew were turning in. When they were turned out to a Road Traffic Collision at 3am, however, the conditions had changed dramatically and the roads were treacherous. Control had told the crew that the incident was near a village called Collaton St Mary, just outside Paignton on the Totnes road. Another appliance was also turned out from Totnes station, coming from the other direction. This is standard practice if the incident is between two station grounds. The Paignton appliance had driven through the village of Collaton St Mary, but as they had not come across the incident, they thought they must have missed it. I must just add that if the police, ambulance or any member of the public give you ambiguous directions, and you then overtake cars with your blues and twos going, it is always a little embarrassing to then be seen by the same cars going back in the opposite direction still under blues and twos. I would like to say that this has never happened to me while I have been in charge of an appliance, but sadly I can't!

Having not come across the accident, this is exactly what the officer in charge decided to do, but the road was too narrow to turn in. He therefore suggested that the driver take a side road, leading down to a fishing lake, in order to turn in the car park at the bottom. I know this road quite well, and it has a very steep hill falling away from it, but I have never driven on it covered in ice, nor would I want to! The crew, however, were committed to turning around, but as it was still dark they were unaware of how icy it was. Despite driving carefully, the driver lost control of the appliance and it started to slide towards the very steep slope, where it would undoubtedly have rolled over and over had it reached the edge. The officer and driver both thought that they were going over, and yelled at the crew to leap for safety on the driver's side of the vehicle. Neither the driver or the officer had a chance to get out, but at the last second the driver regained control and a disaster was narrowly averted, apart from a few bumps and bruises sustained by the crew in the back, who had all leapt for it. Thankfully the appliance was saved and there were no serious injuries.

A LOCK UP COCK-UP!

This incident happened to a friend of mine when he was an officer in charge of a three-pump station in a city on the south coast. As you may recall from the 'maritime museum' story, we do training exercises from time to time in buildings other than fire stations to try and make training as realistic as possible. Breathing apparatus search and rescue drills are much more challenging when the crews are not familiar with the layout of a building, as of course they are not in most fires which we are called to.

So it was that Dave and his second in command, also called Dave, had organised a breathing apparatus drill in a derelict department store (Debenhams were relocating to other premises at the time) in the city centre. Dave 1 had got the key to the empty building, and having risk assessed its suitability for a safe exercise, organised the exercise the next time they went on duty. You will appreciate that when we are doing drills or exercises we have to stay in radio communication with control in order to respond to any emergency calls that might come in. Usually it is a driver that stays on the appliance to answer the radio and also to help with as swift a getaway as possible.

On this occasion the dummies had been hidden in the building and the crews were committed in breathing apparatus to find them. Dave 1 was the officer in charge outside the building and Dave 2 was inside the building as a safety officer and, being a breathing apparatus instructor, he was checking that the teams were using the correct procedures. At the height of the exercise, when all the crews were in the building except for the driver, the entry control officer and Dave 1, a fire call came in. Dave 1 shouted to everyone in the building to get out as there was a fire call and everyone rushed back to the machines. For some reason, however, Dave 2, who was the officer in charge of the second appliance, did not hear the shout or get the message about the fire call, was stuck inside the building. Dave 1, aware of his responsibility to Debenhams and the security of the building, duly locked the door, jumped on his appliance and drove off on 'blues and twos' to the fire at an address on the other side of the city. Dave 2, meanwhile, was firmly locked in the building, but as he was the officer in charge of the second appliance they could not proceed without him! The driver of appliance 2 had to radio through to Dave 1 to get him to turn round and bring the key back to let out Dave 2. It is just so embarrassing when you have to turn round and drive back past the cars you have just overtaken on 'blues and twos' and go back past them in the opposite direction!!!

A BATHROOM BREAK IN

This was one of the earliest 'special service calls' that I attended, and one call out that made me realise that despite our best intentions we do not always get it quite right!

We were called out to the Devonport area of Plymouth, to a high rise block of council flats where an elderly man was stuck in the bathroom. The flat was occupied by two very elderly brothers who we shall call Bob and Bert. Bob had gone into the bathroom for his weekly bath and Bert had got very worried that he had been in there for a very long time and was not responding to his calls, and the door was firmly locked. I should mention here that Bert was about eighty years old and it was his older and very deaf brother that was in the bathroom.

My boss at the time knocked loudly on the bathroom door, but got no response. Fearing that Bob may have either fallen asleep in the bath and might have been drowning, or may have had a heart attack, decided rightly that there was no time to waste and that the door had to be broken down. At the same time he sent someone to get a blanket and the 'Mars' resuscitator. He then turned to Frank who was an ex-Irish guard, six-foot four and fifteen stone, and asked him to break the door down. The corridor in the flat was only about three feet wide but Frank leant back on the other side of the corridor and took a three foot run up and hurled his shoulder at the door. The council door was always going to come off second best and burst inwards.

The bathroom was very small, with the door opening onto the bath which was on the side wall behind the door. Then there was just room for a toilet and basin at the other end. Fortunately for dear old Bob he had neither had a heart attack nor drowned. Unfortunately for him he had snoozed off in the bath and had not heard his brother calling him. He had however been roused by my boss and the noise we were all making. He decided then that it was time to get out of the bath, but the timing could not have been worse, for as he was getting out, Frank was coming in! This resulted in Bob standing behind the door trying to open it as Frank was opening it with his shoulder. As the door opened inwards Bob found himself thrown inwards and back in the bath for the second time. As he looked up in his dazed and bemused state, it was to see the sight of four yellow helmets looking down on him. The sight of his four would-be rescuers who had come to help him, but had just smashed him back into his bath!

RAISING THE ROOF

We frequently get called out to road traffic accidents or collisions as they are now called. We often have to make the vehicles safe in order that they do not catch fire, and often clear up any spillages. In more serious accidents where the driver or passengers in the car may be trapped, we then have to cut or spread the cars apart in order to get the injured persons out. This is quite a skilful process and entails the use of powerful hydraulic cutting equipment that we regularly practice with on cars that are no longer road-worthy.

One other piece of information that needs to be taken in before you can understand this story, is that firefighters often park their cars in other fire station yards if they are visiting another town in order to save car parking charges as we are often located in or near town centres.

This unfortunate incident happened to a friend of mine who used to be in the Hampshire Fire Service. He was based in a Portsmouth station, but had a social event to attend on Hayling Island. He therefore called the station at Hayling and asked if he could park his car in their station yard on the next Friday evening. He was assured that there would be no problem, but perhaps he ought to drop his keys into the watchroom when he arrived.

Just prior to this Friday, my friend had sold his fairly old Ford Cortina to one of the younger members of his watch for a few hundred pounds as it was, to be respectful, a bit past it's prime. The same younger firefighter happened to be going to the same social event and so offered my friend a lift in the Cortina. This he gratefully accepted, and they set off for Hayling on a wet winters Friday evening, but arrived a bit later than intended. Now, being in a bit of a rush, and not seeing any of the Hayling firefighters around, they decided to rush off to their social do. By all accounts they had a great evening, but being a bit the worse for drink, sensibly decided to take a taxi home.

My friend said he would give his young friend a lift back to Hayling to get the Cortina, but could not give him a lift until the Sunday. This was agreed, and so they duly arrived back at Hayling late on the Sunday morning. As they turned into the station yard the new owner of the Cortina was horrified to see that the roof of the Cortina had been completely removed. The Hayling firefighters had just assumed that the fairly old car had been left for them to practice their car cutting up skills.

"It looks like you now have a convertible" said my friend!

Fiery Tales

Fiery Tales

PART 2: 'WIND-UPS'

TIMMY AND TUMMY TROUBLE

MARITIME MUSEUM MISCHIEF

A VIKING LONGSHIP

ALL TIED UP AND NOWHERE TO GO

BACKSIDE ON THE DOCKSIDE

POSTMAN PRAT

THERE'S A ROADSWEEPER ON FIRE

COOKING UP A STORY

I'VE SEEN A GHOST

YOU'RE DRIVING US QUACKERS

BRICKING IT

A WET WELCOME AND A WARM FAREWELL

TIMMY WITH TUMMY TROUBLE

Most 'wind-ups' happen on the spur of the moment, or take only the minimum of planning, but occasionally a little more thought and perseverance results in a much more amusing 'wind up.' Amusing, that is, for those instigating the prank, possibly somewhat less so for the victim. This 'wind up' took the best part of four months, and you will see why as I attempt to explain it to you.

The target was a really good guy from a neighbouring fire station called Tim, who has always battled with his weight. He is not a 'fatty', in fact he is quite a sporty guy, but when not in training, like many of us, he tends to put on a few extra pounds. Towards the end of the summer Tim had a knee injury problem that stopped him running. This time he was determined that he was not going to put on weight. He therefore decided that in the months leading up to Christmas he was going to go over to the gym at work whenever time allowed, and credit where credit is due, this he did religiously. The rest of his watch were soon very aware of how hard he was working on the rowing machine, the exercise bike, and general circuits, and how worried he was about his weight.

After a few weeks of this hard training, he announced to his workmates that he thought he had actually started to lose weight. This was probably a mistake, as it gave one of the practical jokers the glimmer of an idea. The next time Tim went over to the gym in his tracksuit and trainers, the prankster went looking for Tim's work trousers and belt. The buckle on our Fire Service belts is detachable, so our crafty prankster removed the buckle from Tim's belt, snipped about a quarter of an inch (5mm?) off the end of the belt and replaced the buckle. Tim, who was pleased with his work out, was disappointed to find that after a shower and changing back into his trousers, that they felt a little bit tight. The process of snipping a little piece off the belt was repeated every few weeks over a four-month period. At one point Tim even mentioned to the watch that, although he knew he was losing weight, he could not understand why his trousers felt so tight. He even suggested that it might be that his stomach muscles were getting stronger! I know that if he had said that to me, and I had known what was going on, there is no way that I could have kept a straight face, and in fact I would probably have dissolved into fits of laughter.

The 'coup de grace' was finally delivered at the green watch Christmas dinner. The watch commander at the time always sang a carol to the boys after dinner, with the words of each verse doctored cleverly to ' take the Mickey' out of one of the individuals present. Before he sang Tim's verse, Tim was asked to pull a cracker with him. As the cracker pulled apart out fell the eight pieces of belt that had been snipped over the preceding weeks. The rest of the watch predictably erupted into fits of laughter, and poor Tim realised that it was not his increased stomach muscles that were responsible for his tightening trousers!

MARITIME MUSEUM MISCHIEF

Several years ago a large exercise was organised at a maritime museum on the south coast. The purpose of the exercise was threefold. Firstly to do a search and rescue exercise in thick, but entirely harmless, smoke that we generated ourselves. Dummies were placed throughout the building for the firefighters to search for in breathing apparatus, as they would in a real fire scenario. Secondly positive pressure ventilation fans were to be used to force the smoke out of the building. Finally a simulated salvage operation was to take place to see how long it would take to remove the valuable artefacts from one area of the museum. Salvage is something we are very aware of, especially in listed buildings or heritage sites, where it is important to remove the contents from the building as quickly as possible to prevent damage from both fire and water.

The assistant chief of the county concerned, who was very proud of the efficiency and professionalism of his men, oversaw the whole exercise. The curator of the museum was also there to observe proceedings, and was duly impressed and pleased to think that his museum was in such safe hands in the event of an emergency. The dummy casualties were found and rescued in brisk fashion, the smoke was cleared by the fans in very good time and the senior officer was positively bristling with pride. The final stage of the exercise then got underway, and involved the firefighters carrying the contents of one wing of the museum out of the building to a place of safe keeping. This was mainly a logistical exercise to see just how long a salvage operation would take in the event of a real fire.

A line of firefighters proceeded to bring an assortment of items out of the main entrance under the close scrutiny of the assistant chief and the curator. Everything was going extremely smoothly until one firefighter, carrying a large vase, apparently tripped on the doorstep. The vase crashed onto the concrete and smashed into hundreds of pieces at the feet of the curator who was desperately worried as to which piece might have been broken. The assistant chief was almost apoplectic with rage. Unknown to the two of them, however, but known to every other firefighter involved in the exercise, this clumsy firefighter had been to the auction rooms the day before, where he had bought the vase for 50 pence. You can imagine the merriment of all the other firefighters who witnessed his deliberate trip and slip!

A VIKING LONGSHIP

It is commonplace in the Fire Service for firefighters to get a huge amount of pleasure from playing pranks on, and 'winding up', their colleagues. Certainly going back a few years when there was less political correctness and probably more time to spare, these 'wind ups', could become quite elaborate. The danger with winding too many people up too often, of course, is that, as in this story, the pay back can be quite serious.

A well-known prankster and 'Mickey-taker' was stationed at Camels Head Fire Station, which is near Plymouth dockyard, and very close to Weston Mill creek, a tributary of the river Tamar. The prankster, who we shall call Dave, was on duty one night shift, during which they had several fire calls and not very much sleep. At around the same time all fire stations were constantly getting phoned and asked about the fire calls they had received. Normally we have very good relations with the press, but when Dave was phoned at around 7am on the morning of his night shift he was caught in a grumpy mood. When asked about the fire calls they had received during the night, Dave told the earnest young reporter that they had not been very exciting, but that he was surprised that the Western Morning news reporters were not down at Weston Mill creek. On asking "why", Dave told her that the remains of a Viking longship had been discovered in the creek, and that as he spoke the 'Time Team" from channel 4 were investigating. Dave and the rest of the watch were in hysterics when, twenty minutes later, two reporters and a cameraman were to be seen traipsing up the creek.

This story could end there, but there is a twist in the tale that needs to be told. Unknown to Dave, one of the other lads on the watch had a friend who worked on the Western Morning News. He realised that here was a great opportunity to get his own back on Dave. He got a sheet of headed paper from his friend and wrote a fake letter to the Chief Fire Officer, which read roughly as follows:

Dear Sir,
I would like to bring it to your attention that on the morning of 4th May, at approximately 7am, one of our reporters was misinformed by one of your firefighters from Camels Head Fire Station that a Viking longship had been discovered in Weston Mill creek. As this information proved to be

*totally scurrilous, and we sent two reporters and a cameraman to the scene, we suggest that this irresponsible firefighter should pay our costs of £200, and be given a serious reprimand for his childish behavi*our.

To complete the wind-up on Dave, his colleague obtained some headed paper from headquarters, and wrote one more fake letter, to Dave's boss:

Dear Station Officer,
Following the enclosed complaint from the Western Morning News, I would like you to investigate the following matter. When you have found the culprit of this irresponsibility, I suggest that you make him write a letter of apology and enclose a cheque for the £200. Could you also arrange a time to send this firefighter to see me for a severe reprimand?

When Dave returned to work on the following tour of duty he was presented with both letters. On reading them he went ashen white, but none of his colleagues told him for two days that he, of all people, had fallen hook, line, and sinker for this very good wind-up!

ALL TIED UP AND NOWHERE TO GO

Before embarking on the all tied up and nowhere to go story, I am just going to tell you about two food and drink pranks. Normally we respect each other's food and drink, but it never pays to gloat or show off at the fire station. The first food story involves my long time boss and friend Dave. Dave went through a phase of popping into the local bakers before coming to work to get two fresh baked bread rolls. His wife would put a different filling in his lunch box every day, be it ham cheese or whatever. Dave would religiously have one roll at eleven o'clock and the other at lunch time. Before cutting the roll in half to put in the filling, he would always say something like 'ah, fresh bread, you cannot beat it', or 'just smell that gorgeous fresh baked smell'. Whether there was a touch of jealousy or not, I'm not sure, however the rest of his watch got a bit fed up with him always going on about his blooming bread rolls.

One day one of them decided between nine and eleven o'clock that they would sneak up to the kitchen and find Dave's lunch-box. He then got the two rolls out of the box, and with a very sharp knife carefully cut a circle out of the crust at the bottom of the roll. He then pulled out all the fluffy fresh bread from the inside of the roll and replaced it with flour. He did this to both the rolls and then carefully managed to put the bottoms back in so that you could scarcely see that they had been tampered with.

When Dave came up for tea-break at eleven he sat down at the head of table as usual and pulled out one of the rolls. There was eager anticipation around the table as he cut into his roll, as every one but he, knew what was going to happen. As he cut into the roll a big cloud of flour came out, much to everyone else's delight. The strangest thing of all, however, was that Dave did not realise that his rolls had been tampered with. He simply thought that they had been undercooked and was cross with the baker. Nobody enlightened him as to the real reason for the floury centre, and he even went as far as to take the rolls back to the baker to complain!

He admitted to me, that it was not until he was handing the rolls over to the confused baker that he noticed the fine knife cut in the bottom and twigged what had happened too late. He was too embarrassed to admit suddenly that there had been a mistake and even allowed the baffled baker to give him his money back. The baker assured him that nothing like this had happened before…probably not!

The second, drink related story this time, happened to my current boss 'Tuckers', but many years ago. Tuckers used to have a pint sized tea-mug which he used to bring out at all tea-breaks, saying that he liked a good drink of tea and not half a cup. This was all very well, but his watch used to make a tea-pot for all the watch which only just contained enough for all of them. Tuckers always poured himself a very full mug which quite often meant that the last person up for tea, had to make another pot. Not too much of a hardship I agree, but annoying nevertheless. After a period of 'Tuckers' hogging more than his share of the tea the others decided to act. One of the firefighters brought in a high-powered electric drill and drilled a very fine hole right through his mug, just under the handle where it could not be seen. As it was a white mug they then filled the hole with a thick paste made out of cornflour. At the next tea-break Tuckers produced his huge mug that now had a discreet hole bored in it. He filled it to the top and sat down with a smug grin. The rest of the watch sat down with more of an air of expectation. Their little stunt worked even better than they could have hoped, for as 'Tuckers' raised his mug for his first mouthful the paste gave way and a perfect stream of tea was seen to spurt out of his mug below his elbow. Needless to say the oversized mug was never seen again. As I say, it never pays to gloat!

We now move on to possibly the most embarrassing moment in my Fire Service career. I was still a probationer and had to be a bit careful about going to bed before the older hands when we were on night duty. One night however I was particularly tired and decided to risk going to bed while they were still playing cards. I had dropped off into a deep sleep when the card school came and jumped on me and using a cow-net and some lines tied me very securely into my bed.(A cow-net is something we use to help lift larger animals if they get stuck in rivers, bogs, slurry-pits or wherever). Having tied me up, they then carried me downstairs still in my bed and put me in the appliance bay between the two engines. I was worried that I would miss a fire-call if we got one and said so. I was assured that I would be untied if the system went down. Sure enough, not much later we did get a call to a house fire with 'persons reported'. I struggled furiously to get out, but could not, even with the others trying to help me. Due to the seriousness of the call, and as the numbers on duty that night allowed, the boss told them to leave me and they roared off into the night leaving me still securely tied to my bed. Worse still, as the main doors to the fire station were still up anybody walking past could see me in my bed and must have assumed that I was too tired to go on the fire-call. Nothing further from the truth I can assure you.

BACKSIDE ON THE DOCKSIDE

I am sure I have mentioned before that probationer firefighters get quite a lot of stick from the older members of the watch, and I was no exception, although I was a bit cheeky and did try to give some back. In the fire service it is not just the members of your own watch that you come into contact with, and when I was at Camels Head fire station (many years ago) we frequently got called to the Plymouth docks for fire calls, false alarms and exercises which we carried out on Royal Naval ships. Due to the size and nature of the fire risk in the docks we were often turned out with fire appliances from other stations, quite often Crownhill. Obviously you get to know the firefighters from the other stations on the same watch as yourself quite well, and after the calls to the docks there was often time for some good natured banter between the crews, and occasionally a little more!

There was one firefighter from Crownhill, who we shall call 'Blacky', who was an enormous man, and a large character to boot, but was also blessed with a huge pair of ears. Whenever we met, and it was often after a call to the docks, Blacky would always single me out for a bit of good natured abuse. Being much faster on my toes than him, I would often tease him about the size of his ears and then run off before he could catch me. On one such occasion, I had told him what I thought about his ears and then run off and jumped in the back of my own fire appliance. Expecting my own crew to jump in beside me I was horrified when Blacky and one of his equally huge mates jumped in either side of me and proceeded to give me a friendly but painful pummelling from either side. 'Now, what were you saying about my ears, Wolfy?', Blacky asked, and despite my protestations about what a wonderful pair of lugs I thought he had, he told me that he was going to teach me a lesson for being so cheeky.

I know that this will sound ridiculous to some of you, but I can assure you that it is true, that they then forcefully stripped me naked and threw me out of the appliance and into the dockyard. As you can imagine this got more than a few looks from the dockyard workers. As I attempted to get back on the machine as fast as possible to hide my embarrassment, the driver of my appliance drove off towards the dockyard gates. To be fair he only drove about 50 metres, but of course every other firefighter was in hysterics at the sight of me chasing the fire appliance in my nakedness!

Fiery Tales

When I was allowed back in, I tried to dress as fast as possible, but I could not find my pants anywhere. The officer in charge informed me that I was very unlikely to see them again, and I looked up to see where he was pointing. I was just in time to see my underpants disappearing out of the dockyard gate on the aerial of Crownhill's fire appliance, with all their crew leaning out of the window, laughing and waving at me. I must just say here that this sort of behaviour would not be condoned now, or not in a public place anyway!

POSTMAN PRAT

After you have done your three months' training in the Fire Service, you are on probation for two years before becoming fully qualified, or so it used to be. During this two-year period the basic skills you have learnt at training school and on the drill ground get put into practice on the fire ground. The junior officers and older hands that you work with pass on the knowledge and experience that they have acquired over the years to help turn you into a fully effective firefighter.

As a result of their 'greenness', naivety and, to different degrees, respect or deference to the older hands, a probationer is a very easy target for a 'wind up'. Some probationers, however, are more gullible than others. A certain probationer, who had recently joined his new station, found himself on a watch where a small group of the older hands were subtle experts at catching out the new probationer. It is easy to see how your ignorance can make you look extremely stupid if given the wrong advice, but sometimes you should just know better…..this story being a case in point!

The relatively new probationer in question was on one of his earlier call-outs, to a post box on fire. This is usually, as in this instance, just a few wisps of smoke coming out of the letterbox opening after some irresponsible idiot has pushed something burning into the post-box. The fire is usually extinguished with as little water as possible, or even a dry powder extinguisher, in order to avoid further damaging the post any more than necessary, but still ensuring the fire is out. Normal practice is then to contact the post office via control to let them know which post-box has been affected. They will then sort out the resultant mess as best they can.

On this occasion, after putting out the fire, the probationer asked, "what happens now?" Instead of telling him that the post office come to unlock the box, one of the old hands nudged his mate and said with a very straight face, "we unscrew the top". This should have seemed absurd, but for a split second the gullible firefighter looked at the faces of the older hands and momentarily put his hands on the top of the post-box, as if to unscrew it. "No, not that way, anti-clockwise" said one of the older hands, before Postman Prat realised he was making a complete idiot of himself. The gullible probationer didn't actually launch himself at the post-box as depicted by Paul in the illustration, but I have to admit that it was me!

For obvious reasons I have been very reluctant to include this story, but several friends have told me that they were not going to buy the book without the post-box story in it, and I reasoned that you couldn't really laugh at everyone else's gaffes without being able to admit to, and laugh at, your own!

THERE'S A ROAD-SWEEPER ON FIRE!

Following on from the very embarrassing Postman Prat story, this is another story based on a momentary flash of imaginary madness, which I will try to explain.

The firefighter involved had, shortly before the road-sweeper incident, been to a fairly horrific incident that made a vivid and lasting impression on him. He and his crew had been called to an address near a garage where a seriously distressed man had poured a can of petrol over himself and then struck a match, turning himself into a human torch. Could anyone imagine a more horrendous way to commit suicide? When the crew arrived he was 'well-alight', but still alive. He later died in hospital from seventy per cent burns. There is clearly absolutely no humour to be derived from this very sad episode. Sadly it was the second time that this individual had set himself on fire. The person and the hospital will remain anonymous, but this incident had a direct bearing on our story, as will be revealed.

Now, back to our road-sweeper incident. The fire appliance involved was out on other duties when it was called on to attend to a road-sweeper on fire. For some strange reason, perhaps because of the human torch incident, the firefighter concerned had in his mind a picture of a human road sweeper (like Trigger in Only Fools and Horses), with a brush in his hand. In fact, of course, it was the four-wheeled variety, with revolving mechanical brushes, that was actually on fire. No one would ever have known what he was thinking if he had not uttered the words, as they neared the address, which were to haunt him evermore on his watch, "Where is this road sweeper chap, then?". We turned the corner to see the road-sweeping vehicle, full of leaves, on fire, before the reality of the situation became clear to the fire-fighter with the vivid imagination. The rest of the crew were hysterical at his stupid comment and yes, once again I'm afraid it was me!

COOKING UP A STORY

This is a short story about a young man joining the fire service, who had a poor diet, living almost entirely on fried food and 'takeaways', who had almost no idea of how to cook at all. He was also more than a little gullible, as you will see. We shall call him John. No one had ever shown him how to cook, and a short stint in the army, where he was catered for, did not help. After leaving the army he undertook three months' training as a firefighter and turned up on a watch at Exmouth fire-station with virtually no culinary skills whatsoever.

This shouldn't have presented too much of a problem, apart from poor nutrition, except that on some watches you are expected to cook for each other on certain occasions, usually on your second night shift. Many watches in the fire service like to sit down together and enjoy a meal, plus the usual good-natured banter that goes with it. John was on just such a watch, which happened to have a few good cooks who prided themselves on turning out good quality food for each other. After two greasy fry-ups offered by John, his culinary shortcomings were soon exposed, and the rest of the watch decided that something had to be done.

In the fire service we regularly get sent on courses to improve or brush up on our core skills, such as breathing apparatus or road traffic collision courses. We also get sent on several slightly more questionable courses such as 'equality and fairness' or 'risk assessment courses', but I digress. For any course we get sent very formal and detailed joining instructions. The lads at Exmouth got in touch with the person responsible for allocating courses and asked her to make up a basic cookery skills course and send the bogus joining instructions to poor John. For those of you who are astounded at how gullible John must have been to believe that such a course existed, let me assure you that when you are still a probationer and your boss tells you that you are going on a course, and all the watch are in on the wind-up, it is very believable. I enclose overleaf a copy of the joining instructions that John was sent, which I think you'll agree are very believable!

As the joining instructions asked John to turn up at the kitchen at the brigade headquarters in a chef's apron and hat, this is exactly what he did, carrying a pot, a pan and a mixing spoon. Imagine the hilarity of the kitchen staff when John arrived suitably dressed at nine o'clock one morning.

Of course one of his off-duty colleagues was there with his camera to capture the moment. I understand, however, that John took the joke much better than some would have done, and from that day onward endeavoured to improve his cooking skills. I hope he also got the chance to get his own back on his work 'mates'. The chance usually appears if you wait for it.

I'VE SEEN A GHOST

This is another story about a gullible probationer, in this case very gullible!

We occasionally get called to serious house fires, where sadly we are too late to save the occupier or occupiers. In these cases the bodies are usually left in situ in order that scenes of crime and fire investigation officers can try to establish the cause of the fire. When they have done their work the body or bodies are put into body bags and taken to the mortuary. We can be asked to help with the bagging up process, but after they have left the fire ground, we obviously have nothing further to do with the body or body bags. That is what makes this story so unlikely, but as it is true just goes to show how a naïve and gullible probationer can be made to believe anything!

This story relates to a new probationer at a Bristol fire station, whose watch had somehow managed to get hold of a body bag. They put one of our search and rescue dummies into the body bag, which they then put in the back of a station van. The two main perpetrators of the prank then drove into the station yard during a work routine and asked some of the watch, including our probationer, who we shall call Brian, if they could help to get the body out of the van. Of course the rest of the watch were in on the wind-up, but Brian asked why there was a body on station. They came up with some cock and bull story about there being a fire last night, but as the mortuary was not yet open they had brought the body back for safe keeping until it was. This seemed reasonable enough to Brian, who helped put the body bag with the dummy in it into the hose shop.

The officer in charge of the watch (also in on the joke) then came out to ask what on earth a body bag was doing on station. The driver of the van told him that the mortuary was not yet open and that they had been asked to look after the body until it was. The boss made out that he was very unhappy about this and said they should go back to the mortuary immediately. By now Brian was convinced that there was indeed a body in the bag. The watch therefore loaded the body bag back into the van and the driver and his mate drove off out of the gate. Once they had driven round the block, they opened the back of the van and they removed the dummy from the bag. The driver's mate then got into the bag and they dr0ve back to the station.

While Brian was out of the way they hid the dummy out of sight and the driver came in to tell the boss that there is a problem at the mortuary and that they will have to hang on to the body for a few hours. The boss reluctantly agreed and suggested that they put the bag back in the hose shop. Brian helped to carry it in and place it carefully on the floor. As they were walking out of the hose shop, one of the older hands asked Brian if he has seen a body before. Brian said that he hasn't and doesn't particularly want to, but the older hand puts his arm around Brian's shoulder and suggests that, as he is probably going to see many bodies in the course of his career, he probably should check that he can handle it. Brian could see the logic in this, and asked if the corpse was badly burnt, but was told that the body is only slightly blackened by smoke. He reluctantly agreed to go into the hose shop with the older hand. This was the moment that the rest of the watch had been waiting for, and they gradually crept forward to see what was going to happen. Brian, of course, was too engrossed at the grisly prospect of seeing his first body to take any notice of them.

As Brian unzipped the body bag the firefighter who had been patiently waiting for his big moment leapt up out of the bag, scaring Brian half out of his wits, and he in turn leapt backwards in shock. This was exactly the reaction the rest of the on-looking watch were hoping for. I have to say that I think this was a pretty cruel hoax, but an extremely well executed one.

YOU'RE DRIVING US QUACKERS!

I am sure we can all relate to annoying noises such as chalk on the blackboard, squeaky balloons, children shrieking, dogs yapping, or even violins played badly. Talking of musical instruments being played badly, Dave Crawford, the Fire Service Benevolent Fund representative for our area, who wrote the appeal for the charities at the front of this book, and who may have featured in 'Don't be a dummy', learnt to play the bagpipes many years ago. He now plays them very well, but when he was first learning, he used to practice at the fire station, and it made a horrible noise! He not only used to practice when we could all get away from the noise, but also used to wake us up at some ungodly hour of the morning after a night duty, which I am sure you can imagine is not the most soothing way to start the day after a broken night's sleep when you are already irritable! It was, however, a sure fire way for the junior officer to get us out of our beds very quickly indeed.

Another firefighter who used to irritate his colleagues with annoying noises was a chap called Gilly (also the officer in the Timmy with Tummy trouble story), who used to blow a gazoo far too frequently. If he was in a particularly irritating mode he used to creep up behind his mates and blow the gazoo loudly in their ears. Eventually everyone on his watch got completely fed up this, so one day they decided to jump first on Gilly to get his gazoo off him, and then jump on the gazoo so it would never be blown again. Sadly for his watch, this only provided a temporary respite, as Gilly went out and bought an even more irritating noise maker, namely one of those duck decoys which make a horrible, and quite loud, quacking noise. This was even more annoying than the gazoo, so much more fun for Gilly. He quickly realised that, as it was driving the rest of the watch mad, he would have to be very careful that the 'quacker' would not suffer the same fate as the gazoo, so he would only blow it when he had the chance to run away again and hide it. He was warned by his watch that if they ever caught him with his quacker they were going to shove it very firmly 'where the sun doesn't shine'!

Gilly realised that they could be serious, so to save the quacker and the potentially painful prospect of having it rammed up his derriere, he wisely decided to give it to a friend on a different fire station in the city (he was then a firefighter in a different brigade) Unfortunately for his watch, this fire brigade had a tannoy communications link from station to station. Therefore Gilly only had to phone his friend, and at a pre-arranged signal the horrible quacking sound would come out over the tannoy. Gilly, of course, was nowhere to be found, and his watch didn't realise that it was not even Gilly who was blowing the infernal quacker. Thus their threat was never carried out, but I think Paul has excelled himself in his interpretation of what might have been…if only!

BRICKING IT

This story illustrates the extraordinary lengths to which firefighters will go to wind each other up. It revolves around the locker of a firefighter called Scott. Lockers are, as you can imagine, where we keep our spare uniforms and personal effects, and as such it always pays to leave your locker firmly locked! Scott is a great guy, but a serious prankster and occasionally a bit over exuberant, and this is a case in point. He was playing rugby for our brigade team against our bordering county's team, and it was turning into a bit of a grudge match. As it was late in the afternoon and we were on duty we took the fire appliance to the rugby ground to give our support. As we were on call the driver stayed on the machine to answer the radio whilst the rest of our crew walked around the pitch to join the other spectators and give as much vociferous support as possible. During half time, while the teams were having their oranges, our appliance got a fire call, so we trundled across the pitch as fast as possible to get back to the machine. Scott, on seeing me run past his team huddle, could not resist leaping out of the huddle and giving me a full-on waist high tackle, sending me sprawling to the ground in my fire-kit, which I had put on to keep warm. The teams and spectators were hugely amused to see me flattened, but although as an ex-rugby player I have definitely been tackled harder, I was not expecting this and it hurt more than just my dignity. So although this incident is long forgiven, if not forgotten when my back twinges, I could not resist including this story about Scott getting his comeuppance from red watch!

Scott had been at the centre of a lot of wind-ups, which involved other members of the watch having various unwanted items found in their lockers. The watch decided that while Scott was away for a day they would get the spare key for his locker and tamper with it for revenge. Firstly they boarded his locker up with fibreboard, which they screwed onto some wood that they had wedged into the length of his locker. They then removed all the screws and filled in the holes. Thus, when Scott came back to work and went to open his locker, he was presented with the spectacle of a solid board wall in front of his face, much to the amusement of the rest of the watch. This, however, was only the warm up for the 'piece de resistance', as Scott went into retaliation mode and everything started to escalate, as it can on 'playful' watches.

I must say here, and I know it will not make me over popular with some on red watch, but in the past this watch had a bit of a reputation for being a bit union orientated and possibly not working any harder than they had to. This will have changed now, of course, but the station officer at the time told me he had never seen the watch working so hard or in such unison as when Scott next went on leave. His locker was taken out into the yard, where other members of the watch had brought in a cement mixer, bricks, sand and cement. They then make a perfect job of bricking up the front of his locker. The wall was then rendered and painted, and the locker was returned to its rightful place. This all took place over the two days and two nights of a shift. The hugely anticipated moment of Scott opening his locker for the first time on his next tour of duty is recorded for posterity on video, but we can only enjoy Paul's interpretation of the event!

I ought to add here, that the locker that was so wantonly destroyed by red watch's pranksters, was in fact due for replacement.

A WET WELCOME AND A WARM FAREWELL

It has long been a tradition on Fire Stations that any new member of a watch, especially if a probationer, gets a good ribbing and usually a good soaking when they first join their new watch. Even now, in an era of over the top 'political correctness', it would seem wrong not to welcome a new recruit in the time honoured fashion with a good hosing down.

When I joined my first watch, the initial soaking was a well-rehearsed procedure. Immediately after the first parade on duty, the officer in charge of the watch instructed the new recruit, in this instance me, to put on their best uniform ready for the watch photograph. Despite my misgivings of some skulduggery, I was told to get a chair and sit at the base of the brick drill tower, which would give a suitable backdrop to the photograph. While I was changing into my best uniform, two other members of the watch had climbed up inside the tower with a dustbin two thirds full of water. Right on the cue of 'Smile, please' from the officer taking the photograph, the water was tipped directly over my head by my two new colleagues. They, of course, could not miss the sitting target, and the officer taking the photograph was always pleased if he could get the smile and the oncoming cascade of water in the same frame!

After two years at my first station, during which time I had endured many a soaking, and I am pleased to say given many back, I was posted to a station nearer home. Leaving a watch, much like joining one, is another excuse for a bit of horseplay, and quite often for a drink too, but that is another story. On my last night at my first station I was expecting some action, but I have to say my watch excelled themselves! During drills I was tied up and hosed down as expected. Not so expected was to be stripped off and then locked out of the station for what seemed like the best part of half an hour. It was a summer evening, but when I was finally let in to the drying room, I was pretty cold and most of the fight had gone out of me. I was therefore pretty helpless when I was jumped on again, and this time tied to a chair. Still naked, I had my left foot and one of the legs of the chair put into an empty bucket. Imagine my surprise when a bag of plaster was put into the bucket, and water added to set the plaster off. The exothermic reaction was not quite hot enough to burn my leg, but was surprisingly hot all the same.

When the plaster had set firm I was untied, but could not go very far as both my left foot and the leg of chair were held firm in the bucket. After a good deal of struggling I managed to get the chair leg out of the plaster, and finally the plaster mould came out of the bucket. At various stages in this process the rest of the watch came down to laugh and enjoy the spectacle. I was now relatively free, but still had a bucket-shaped lump of plaster on my foot. My only course of action was to drag the lump of plaster on the end of my leg into the appliance bay. Here, still naked, I found a hammer and chisel and took a considerable time to chip myself free.

In retrospect, this behaviour does seem a bit over the top, and I think it unlikely that these sorts of pranks are now as commonplace as they were then. Perhaps most readers would be pleased and reassured to think that this level of horseplay is dying out, but I know a few die-hard old firefighters that regret the passing of such times.

Fiery Tales

PART 3: BOTTOMS UP

BOTTOMS UP

HAVE A DRINK ON ME

FULL STEAM AHEAD

WHO PULLED THE PLUG OUT?

DON'T BE A DUMMY

TABLE IN TROUBLE

WHAT A CRAPPY WEEKEND!

RAT RETRIEVAL

WATCH 'OOT' THERE'S A JOCK 'ABOOT'

THE RED WATCH REBELS

NOT WHAT A NAPKIN RING IS FOR!

THE APPENDIX!

BOTTOMS UP!

Back in the good old days of being a firefighter, when the occasional alcoholic beverage was not quite so badly frowned on, two fire crews attended a pub in South Devon where there had been a strong smell of burning. Non-fire service personnel will probably imagine that fires are always easy to locate, but this is not always the case. They can be in roof spaces, wall partitions, hearths, or even, as in this case, under the floor boards!

The public-house in question had recently been taken over by a new landlord and landlady who were in the middle of promoting their pub in one of the strangest ways I have ever heard of. To boost local trade and to try and create a very friendly atmosphere (intimate even) the main push of their campaign was to issue key-rings to new customers which said 'I've had my bum bitten at the Crown and Sceptre'. The key-rings were only issued to men who had allowed the landlady to bite them on the bum, or ladies (is that the right word?) who had allowed the landlord to bite theirs… interesting sort of pub!

On this particular evening the two crews walked in to be greeted by the very genial host, who counted the firefighters in and then pulled the appropriate number of pints, the fire obviously not being very serious. The officer in charge was a Methodist and tee-total and being very serious minded and extremely conscientious was not at all happy about his men drinking on duty. However he was persuaded to turn a blind eye by his second in command as one pint could not do too much harm and the fire must be nearly out.

Eventually the smell of burning was found to have come from under the floorboards, where a cigarette end or match must have slipped down between a gap in the floorboards and set light to some dust and rubbish. The officer in charge had ordered his men to take up some floorboards to check the fire was completely out and assess the damage. The landlord, much relieved, was now pulling the crew a second pint and was not taking no for an answer. There was by now a very relaxed and gregarious atmosphere developing, and at around the same time one of the firefighters came across the key-rings.

The landlady was only too keen to give out a few more key-rings to those firefighters that thought having their bums bitten was a bit of a laugh. The firefighter who told me this story was at home with his wife when he related it to me. She assured me that Dave came home with definite tooth marks on his backside after the night of this incident, and it took some explaining at the time! However back to the Crown and Anchor, where our very strict officer in charge is having a final look under the floorboards himself. This necessitated his bottom being stuck up in the air. Egged on by some of the other firefighters the landlady saved her best bite for last and really sunk her teeth in to his raised backside. Unfortunately for her, he thought it was one the crew messing around and lashed back over his head with his torch and caught her full in the face with it. That was probably the last bottom she bit without asking first!

The officer in the story retired many years ago, but I feel I must point out that not long after this incident he was awarded the George Medal for pulling a lady from a burning building. It's not all fun and frolics!

HAVE A DRINK ON ME!

This story goes back to the days when many of the larger whole time stations had social clubs and well stocked bars. The bar was usually only opened up on Saturday evenings or on special social occasions and there was nearly always a keen and willing bar manager who took pride in his bar. The profits from the bar were usually put back into the social club to help pay for televisions and other luxuries that improved station life. I know that on the stations where I have worked there has often been a bar representative each with their own key and all very conscientious about keeping the stock in order and the profits as high as they could be. Some watches, however did not want to be involved and they obviously did not have a key.

Before I continue, I feel at this juncture that I must point out that in my experience most firefighters are generally honest, and by the nature of their job generally care about others in the community, so I was not sure about including this story, but it happened a long time ago, so here goes. On this one particular station there was a thriving social club that made good profits from the bar as it was generally very well run. Due to the need for security the bar door had a very secure lock and a very strong metal grill shutter that you could see through, but definitely not get through. There were three bar reps on red, green and white watch but blue watch did not want the responsibility or involvement.

One winter, the bar manager gradually became aware that the spirits in the optics appeared to be going down faster than they should have been and the bar profits were slipping. All watch reps were asked to be vigilant and keep their eyes open, but they were all sure that no one was giving drinks away, but the problem persisted. Eventually by marking the bottles the bar manager was fairly sure that the spirits were going down while blue watch were on duty, which was a bit of a mystery as they did not have access to a key and the bar manager was sure that there was no way into the bar at all without a key. How then were the spirits going down?

Having double checked the marks on the bottles one evening before blue watch came on duty, then checking them again in the morning after blue watches night duty, the drinks had definitely gone down. He was extremely cross, but also exasperated as he could not see how it was possible for anyone to get in or out of the bar. He therefore decided to go into the bar the next evening before blue watch came on duty and laid down in the dark with a book and a torch to see what would happen. He must have been a patient man, because he had to lie there fully three hours before blue watch settled down for the evening. When some of them came into the room he lay motionless and silent to await developments. Some of the blue watch members started a game of snooker, the bar doubling up as the snooker room, and then one of them said "right who's for a drink then". The bar manager tensed, still not having a clue what was going to happen. "I'll have a vodka please Bert". He was then amazed as the spider rest for the snooker cue was pushed through one of the openings of the metal grill with a small tumbler cleverly attached to the end of it. The tumbler was then placed under the optic, and the rest was used to push the tumbler up underneath the optic twice to obtain a double shot of vodka which was then carefully pulled back through the grill and downed in one. " Right who's next?" The bar manager lay there while the rest and tumbler were used to obtain several more doubles. Whilst being blazing wild with blue watch, he could not help but be impressed with their ingenuity.

He then leapt to his feet yelling "you bar stewards", or something very similar! Blue watch were caught red-handed, and admitted that what had started out as being a bit of a laugh and a challenge, was also theft. They agreed to replenish the stock and never use the spider rest again, for anything other than snooker. This promise was in exchange for an assurance that the matter would not be taken to a senior officer. Thus all was well that started badly. It must be said here that although I would not condone blue watches sneakiness in any way, you have to have a begrudging respect for their problem solving ability. The bar manager must surely get a mention too, for lying in wait all that time to catch the culprits!

FULL STEAM AHEAD

Many Fire Services on the coast, and especially those with a port of any reasonable size, have their own fireboats to help counter the risk of fires in ships or on the dockside. This story has only just come to my notice, although it happened over twenty years ago. I was talking to a colleague at my station and reminiscing about having worked in Plymouth, and the old fireboat came up in conversation. It transpired that, as he was ex-navy, he trained to become a coxswain of the fireboat and in fact was one for many years.

I asked if he had been a coxswain when we had the old 'Cissy Brock', which was a huge old tug-boat that had been purchased from the London Fire Brigade and converted into a fire boat. He admitted, with his eyes raised to the sky, that he had been. I understood the expression because, as a firefighter in Plymouth, I had been out on the Cissy Brock several times. I had always been very impressed with the huge pumps that had been fitted, which threw out huge jets of water, but I was never quite so impressed with her speed, because she didn't really have any! If she was called to a fire, as long as it was close by, she could throw an impressive amount of water onto it, but if the fire was very far away, the time taken to get there was interminable. Apparently in her latter years she got even slower, much to the embarrassment of all those who crewed her before she was replaced.

This came up in conversation with the ex-coxswain, a Geordie and a character to boot. He told me that he was crewing the Cissy Brock when they were called to a fire on a boat a little way up the river Tamar. They were chugging away, full steam ahead, when from over the side he heard the word 'pull'. He looked over to see two young lads skulling up the river faster than they were chugging. The situation was not helped when one of the lads suggested that if they were given a bucket of water they would get there first. They got a swift Geordie reply, 'Why don't you just …..off?' I'll give you a clue, it started with f, and ended with k, but I think the Geordies always pronounce it with an 'oo' sound rather than a 'u', which somehow makes it sound funnier, especially in the middle of a river in Devon!

WHO PULLED THE PLUG OUT?

Following on from 'the full steam ahead' story, another rather sad tale regarding the Cissy Brock was of a firefighter, who shall remain nameless, whose pride and joy was the old 'CB'. He used to lovingly take care of the old boat and spend hours cleaning and polishing it. It was regularly moored at a specific place on the harbour wall that gave easy access to the crews, and was also strategically as close as possible to all the risks.

The boat had a routine service one day, which involved the engines and the bilges. This was overseen by our friend, the boat loving firefighter, and at the end of the day all was squared away and everybody left. On return the next day, our friend was horrified to see only the aerial sticking out of the water. Somebody had left the bilges open, and she had gone straight to the bottom of the harbour!

DON'T BE A DUMMY

Firefighters often find themselves hanging around waiting for something to happen. The obvious example is at the Fire Station, where there can be large chunks of time between fire-calls. Another is when you are waiting for a key-holder to turn up to premises you have been called to. Being Firefighters, often restless and impatient, and nearly always 'game for a laugh', this is a situation where high jinks and pranks can occur.

One evening, at around pub throwing-out time, a crew were sent to a ladies' clothes shop, where it was thought that a fire alarm had activated. Quite often, if there doesn't initially appear to be a fire, we will wait outside and ask our control to contact the key-holder of the premises, so that we don't have to cause any damage by breaking in. At night it is often more difficult to ascertain if there is a fire, and if the key holder doesn't come fairly promptly, or if there is any doubt, we will break in rather than risk the possibility of a fire developing.

On this occasion the high street shop was not too easy to get into, so the officer in charge sent a crew around the back to try and gain entry. There was an outer glass door that was open and an inner wooden door that was locked, so the officer-in-charge ordered the wooden door to be broken into. One of the crew took a sledgehammer to the wooden door, and on his back swing completely smashed the glass door, although he did at least gain entry. After entering the shop, it transpired that it was just a burglar alarm sounding, but the crew now had to wait for the key-holder because the premises were insecure, and we also needed to apologise for breaking the glass door!

The crew were informed that the key-holder was going to be a long time coming, so the Leading Firefighter in charge, who is always game for a jolly jape, had noticed a very large, wide brimmed purple hat with an equally large feather in it. He could not resist modelling it, and when it made the lads laugh, he took it one stage further and put on the equally large purple coat that matched it. One of the boys suggested that he should try standing in the shop front window to see if anyone passing would notice. Doing just that, he stood as still as possible amongst the mannequins in the shop window to see what would happen. As luck would have it, the first people to pass the shop window were a pair of drunks staggering home after one too many. One of them spotted the strange looking 'dummy' and beckoned his mate over for a closer look. Our very experienced prankster waited motionless until our two friends had got right up close to the window before he leapt forwards and frightened the living daylights out of them. One of the drunks, at the sight of this horrible apparition lunging towards him, leapt backwards so quickly that he tripped and found himself spread-eagled on his backside on the pavement!

TABLE IN TROUBLE

For those of you not in the Fire Service, in order to understand this story, you need to know that on most whole time stations we have four watches: red, blue, white and green. At change of watch the officer in charge tells the oncoming watch officer anything important that he needs to know. The drivers also tend to hand over to their counterpart on the oncoming watch details about any missing equipment and whether the appliance is in need of fuel. We even had a 'handover' book, so that one watch can let the other watches know any perceived problems. This system has been superseded by e-mail and the electronic exchange of information. However, as with all organisations, this exchange of information is not always perfect, as will be graphically illustrated in this story!

Several years ago we were in the middle of an industrial dispute which resulted in us going out on strike, the rights and wrongs of which I will not dwell on here. At about the same time a firefighter on red watch had a Queen Anne table that needed some restorative work. It was actually his wife's table, a precious heirloom that had recently been left to her by her mother. There was another firefighter, on white watch, who loved antiques and was quite handy at French polishing. The firefighter on red, who we shall call Dave, asked the firefighter on white, who we shall call Nick, if he could help restore the table. Nick said he would be only too happy to have a look at it, and asked Dave to bring it into the station.

Dave duly brought the table in for Nick to have a look at, and Nick said he could help restore it. He suggested that if Dave left it in the hose-shop, out of the way, he would rub and polish it when he was on night duty next. Dave was delighted and duly left the table in the hose-shop. Between red and white shifts my old friends on blue watch came on duty, but unfortunately neither red nor white had mentioned to blue the reason for the old table being in the hose-shop. I mentioned earlier that this was all happening around the time of the strike. What I did not say was that on night duties the striking firefighters were not allowed into the station, so they generally sat outside the station gathered round a nice hot brazier.

To keep this brazier going all through the night required an awful lot of wood, mostly in the form of pallets. I am guessing that you are already way ahead of me. Dear old blue watch were running short of wood for the brazier, so the watch officer suggested that they scout around to see what they could find. No one on blue knew anything about the table, and they wrongly assumed that it had been brought in to be chopped up for firewood. You might have thought that the ornate legs would have made them think twice, but no, out with the axe and into the brazier went the Queen Anne table! The next morning, when Dave came in for his turn of strike duty, one of the chunkier parts of a table leg was still sticking up out of the brazier, but it was not until he went to the hose-shop that the full horror of blue watch's carelessness became apparent.

The story is actually a very sad one, as it was apparently one of the few things to be left to Dave's wife, and the only important heirloom. She, as you can imagine, was furious. The situation was made worse because, although blue watch apologised profusely, Dave later heard them laughing about it, which certainly did not help the situation.

Fiery Tales

WHAT A CRAPPY WEEK-END!

This is another story that you would like to think could not happen in this day and age, and certainly one that you would not want to be involved in yourself! However it did happen to one poor chap in London many years ago, when mobile telephones were not the norm and shops actually closed for bank holidays.

The poor chap concerned had gone shopping in a department store late in the day on a bank holiday Saturday. After completing his purchase from the top floor at about 5.28, he took the lift down to the ground floor in order to get out of the store on time. Unfortunately for him the lift stuck half way down between floors. Worse still, security did not do their checks very thoroughly, and he was still in the lift when the store closed and everyone had gone home. The alarms were not working, and he had no way to contact the outside world. Being stuck in a lift for a few hours can seem interminable, so you can imagine the depths of his despair when he was stuck there until the following Tuesday morning!

We frequently get called to shops, hotels and anywhere that has lifts in order to help get people out when they get stuck. We have special 'lift keys' to open the doors, and if the lift is completely out of power, and stuck between floors, we can manually wind the lift cage up or down to the nearest floor. In this instance the Fire Service were not called until 8.30 on the Tuesday morning after the bank holiday Monday, so the poor chap concerned had been in the lift for over 60 hours!

The London firefighter who described this incident to me, told me that when they made contact with the man in the lift, he was almost beside himself with rage and desperate to get out in more ways than one. As soon as the lift door was opened he just pushed past them, desperate to get something to eat and drink, and desperate to be anywhere but in that lift. Of course he had not been able to 'hang on' for 60 hours, and the lift was in a terrible mess, which must have made his time in there even more unbearable.

I did say to Paul that I felt this was not really the subject matter for a cartoon, but he asked if he could at least attempt an illustration to depict the horrible scene that would have greeted the rescuers. In his own inimitable style he has come up with the most revolting drawing imaginable. When he first showed me the pencil drawing the man in the drawing was only up to his waist in it!

RAT RETRIEVAL

I am sure I have mentioned elsewhere that, by the very nature of our job, we sometimes have chunks of time to kill. Perhaps I should have said "did" have time to kill, as now, with community fire safety projects and the like, there is certainly less time to entertain yourselves. Perhaps also when you read this story you might think it a good thing that we have less time for "pranks" and "messing" around! But as these pretty irresponsible pranks are becoming more and more a thing of the past, let the stories be told before we become too Politically Correct!

I have seen at first hand the use of the "fake rat" on the end of a nearly invisible length of fishing line. The rat is placed on the opposite side of the street to the Fire Station, and when a suitable pedestrian comes along it is wound in very quickly, giving the impression of a real rat scampering across the road and disappearing into the Fire Station. This caused huge amounts of childish hilarity to the bored Firefighters peering out of the station windows.

At one station near the town centre the rat trick became legendary, with rats Mark 1 and Mark 2 looking ever more realistic, to the point that Ratty might take the occasional outing during the day and still fool the odd pedestrian. This station even invented "the self-righting rat", which had a tummy made out of part of a plastic milk bottle with lead weights in it, such that it would always run across the road the right way up and not on its back or side as some previous models.

At this station there were some self-imposed ratty rules, e.g. no frightening frail old ladies or small children, or not to be used when the road was too busy. However, practical jokes often end up getting a bit out of hand, and after Ratty had nearly been responsible for causing a road traffic accident, when two cars swerved to avoid it, the police suggested quite firmly that Ratty had made his last appearance. The number of laughs created by Ratty's excursions across the road, and his rapid disappearances back into the Fire Station, will long be remembered. The number of people that used to knock on the station door and tell the Firefighters that they had a rat on station takes some believing, and how they ever kept straight faces and said, "Thank you, we'll look out for it" is even more remarkable

One of Ratty's escapades bears special mention. I think it was self-righting Ratty, or certainly one that had a lot of time and effort spent on it. Ratty had been placed across the road one evening and, as boredom had begun to set in, the rules started to be broken. Ratty was running back across the road when he became snagged on something and, when tugged, he jumped up and became stuck in the radiator grille of an oncoming bus. Ratty was free and off down the road to the great consternation of all concerned. Was that to be the end of Ratty? No, the duty driver was sent off in the van in hot pursuit of the bus, and the next time the bus pulled in to allow more passengers on, the van pulled in behind it. The duty driver nipped out smartly, retrieved Ratty without any undue ceremony, even a degree of nonchalance, and took him safely back to his home station.

I am sure that many readers will be pleased to hear that this sort of silliness does not go on any more, or at least not as often. I know that some watches in particular at the station concerned were notorious for their horseplay. In fact the Firefighter, now nearly retired, who told me this story, admitted that, as a much younger Firefighter, he had once been strapped into a paraguard stretcher. That is not so terrible in itself, but he was then stripped from the waist down and hung up in the station window for all passers-by to see. Of course not everybody looked in. but they tended to when the other members of his watch took it in turns to knock on the window and attract their attention!

WATCH 'OOT', THERE'S A JOCK 'ABOOT'

One of my ex-bosses, now retired, was a Scotsman, and a bit of a character to boot. He was a very conscientious Fire Officer, who always stuck up for his men, but he called a spade a spade. He was also a staunch union man with quite a fiery temper, and he did not suffer fools lightly. I only outline some of his character traits as they are relevant to the story.

Despite living in England for many years he still had a very strong Scottish accent, which caused us some moments of amusement when we were interacting with the public. I remember one occasion when we got called to a house with a chimney on fire. The lady owner of the house was quite a correct and well-spoken English lady who was having a little trouble with his accent. He kept referring to the 'soot' up the chimney being the cause of the fire, but in broad Scottish he pronounced it as 'suit'. The lady in question turned to me and asked why he kept talking about 'suits' and was there anyone on the crew who could speak English. Trying to contain myself I suggested that perhaps I should take over with the communications on this incident!

We now come to the incident that sticks in my mind as being a good illustration of the strength of his character. The police had called us, in the early hours of a Sunday morning, to help get a drunken Saturday night reveller down from a roof in the town centre. He had climbed out of his flat window and was walking along above a glass-covered pavement area, where he was a danger not only to himself but also to anyone walking underneath. The police did not have the ladders to go up to get him down, which was where we came in.

We pitched the ladder and looked at the two young constables, who seemed very reluctant to go up themselves. I didn't blame them, as the drunk was carrying on and being verbally abusive. My boss suggested that he would go up himself, and the two policemen agreed only too readily. He then turned to me and said, "Up we go, then", which was not quite how I had envisioned it. I was quite happy to stay at the bottom of the ladder and foot it. However, he was not someone you could argue with, and up we went. When we got up to the hooded youth, who seemed a bit surprised to see two firefighters and not the police, my boss went straight up to the youth and gave him two options. "Right" he said, "you can do this the hard way or the easy way". The youth looked confused. My boss clarified things. "You either walk down the ladder yourself, or I knock you out and Pete here will carry you down the ladder."

The lad took one look at him, and very wisely took the easy option and walked down the ladder with me behind him, much to my relief. When we got to the ground and handed the lad over to the police they were very impressed at such a straightforward outcome. They asked my boss what he had said. He replied, "It's not what you say, but the way that you say it!" How true; the lad took only a second to realise that he meant exactly what he said. Sadly we cannot now condone this type of action, but I for one sometimes regret that things are not as simple as they used to be!

THE RED WATCH REBELS

I am currently working with a colleague who used to be in the London Fire Brigade. We call him the crafty cockney, and he often makes me laugh with his sharp wit and tales from his days in 'sin city'. It would be a shame not to include some of his stories, although many are not printable! Here are two that made me chuckle in different ways.

He was on red watch and admits that they were a bit wild, especially in their time off, but sometimes on duty as well. They tended to do their own thing and not get too involved with the other watches, which did not make them overly popular, although they played on this a bit and sometimes just said "no" on principle. A case in point was when the other watches decided to get together and make a really nice garden out of some spare land at the side of the station. Green watch took the lead role and designed the garden, and organised the other two watches into doing their share of the work. Red watch, he admits, did absolutely nothing.

After a few months this garden looked fantastic, with flower beds beautifully planted out and a nice decked area to sit on. The other watches were so cheesed off with red watch's lack of involvement that they did not even want them to sit in the garden. Shortly after the garden was finished, a member of the public saw what a good job they had done and mentioned it to the local press. A journalist asked if he could come and take a photograph of the garden and write a short piece about it. Unfortunately he phoned the station when red watch were on duty. They readily agreed that the press could come round later that day. The whole watch, who had not lifted a finger between them, came out into the garden and posed for the camera leaning on shovels or holding trowels, giving the impression that they had been solely responsible for the lovely garden. The officer on green watch was apoplectic with rage when he saw the picture in the paper of red watch in 'his' garden, apparently taking all the credit for it!

The other story that is printable concerns the time they went to a fire in a clothes shop, and someone came back to station with the slightly charred leg of a shop dummy. I can think of all sorts of things that this might have been used for, but they decided to use it as a baseball bat. This doesn't sound too irresponsible until you factor in that they decided to play indoors in the mess-room, using billiard balls! My friend was batting when he hit one billiard ball clean through the window of the station officer's office. He, being a 'Mr. Grumpy', was very unlikely to see the funny side of red watch playing baseball indoors, so the boys had to swing into action. They took the beading for his window out, removed the window with the perfectly circular hole in it and replaced it with the same size window from the kitchen door. That seemed understandable to me, but I could not understand why they then put the window with the hole in it back into the kitchen door! Crafty explained to me that the kitchen door was always propped open against the wall, so was much less likely to be seen with a hole in it. Again, I must emphasise that it is highly unlikely that anyone would be found on station now playing baseball indoors with a shop dummy's leg!

NOT WHAT A NAPKIN-RING IS FOR!

I wasn't sure if this was the right material for a supposedly humorous book, but when I saw Paul's drawing I knew that it had to be included!

We regularly get called to cut rings off people's fingers, as we have a very good ring-cutting implement, which is simply a hand powered circular saw blade that cuts against a metal back. It is obviously nothing like the powered circular saw as depicted by Paul. Most Fire Stations have a ring-cutter in their first aid boxes, so members of the public come in occasionally to have their rings removed.

A few years ago we were asked to go to the accident and emergency ward of the local hospital to assist with the difficult removal of a graphite ring from a young boy's finger. The poor lad was in so much pain that the doctor in charge had to anaesthetise him so that we could carry on cutting off the ring before he lost his finger. Thus it was that I found myself in full firefighting kit in an operating theatre at the hospital. Thankfully the ring was eventually removed after we had purchased a very small electrical circular cutter.

This leads us on to the slightly less pleasant task that we sometimes get asked to help with, namely the removal of rings from other appendages. Not long after the incident with the boy, we were called to the hospital to assist with the removal of a napkin ring from a man's penis. The ring had been on there for some time before he was brought into the hospital, and his appendage was starting to go a deep red, going on purple, colour. Just to add to the man's embarrassment, we had with us a female firefighter, who despite being quite broad minded got a bit of a shock when she stepped into the cubicle!

This story would not have come to print if it were not for the fact that I mentioned it to another watch a few weeks later. I was amazed to hear that they had been called to the hospital to help the same man, with the same problem, just a different napkin ring! It is probably not for me to comment on how anybody should 'entertain' themselves. However I cannot leave the story without asking the obvious question, 'why did he not learn his lesson from the first experience?' Apparently his penis was in a worse state this time, having gone from a red-purple colour to more of a purple-black colour. I apologise to the more sensitive among you, but I feel without the colours you cannot begin to imagine how gross this was!

THE APPENDIX

This is not strictly speaking a Fire Service story, but one that involved off duty Fire Service personnel, and which nearly had some serious repercussions for the Fire Service. I was renovating a small two up, two down property that only had a lean-to shack for a kitchen. The first job was to knock the old kitchen down and clear some space to build a new kitchen. As we were clearing the old kitchen out, a few items left by the previous occupier, that looked like they might be useful, were being moved out of the old shack and back into the dining room area adjacent to it. On of these items was a glass container that we all assumed contained sugar, so we put it next to the kettle ready for use. Yes, you are right, being members of the Fire Service we should be more careful about chemical substances!

As the final walls were coming down there were a lot of wires sticking out that needed to be disconnected. The builder I was working with suggested that we get an electrician in as soon as possible to disconnect the wires that were making demolition awkward. I telephoned an off-duty firefighter who is also a qualified electrician, and he said he would be there in the afternoon as soon as he could. When he arrived he spotted the kettle, as all workmen do, and asked if he could have a cup of coffee as he was gasping. I made a drink for us all, but he was the only one who wanted sugar in his coffee (two spoonfuls). He also asked for his coffee milky so that he could drink it quickly and get on with his electrics.

As soon as he got his mug he gulped two mouthfuls straight down, before the taste hit him and too late to spit it out. "God, what was that Wolfy?" "Sorry mate, I really thought it was sugar". We made him wash his mouth out with copious amounts of water, but to this day we do not know what the substance was, although it certainly did not feel right in his stomach. That night he went to work, but the following day he was admitted to hospital with griping stomach pains. The following night his officer telephoned me to ask what he had swallowed as the hospital wanted to know. Now I was seriously worried that I was responsible for poisoning him!

What I did not know at the time was that he had been having some serious stomach pains on and off. When I next telephoned the hospital to ask after him I was told that he had been operated on and had a perforated appendix removed. The next time I spoke to him he told me that, although the substance had not helped, the doctors had told him that his appendix had been in a mess for a long time, and that his life may have been saved by the doctors searching deeper. Phew, what a result. The rumour had gone around the Fire Service that 'Wolfy' had poisoned his friend. What a turn around we had, from zero to hero for a change! However, I am now extremely careful what I put in anybody's coffee, and my watch do not even let me make the tea any more!